ABOUT AUTHOR

Kamlesh Vishwakarma is a seasoned professional in the field of Amazon marketing, renowned for his extensive years of experience and expertise in ecommerce. As an Amazon-verified Advertising Partner, he showcases his credibility and proficiency in online advertising. Kamlesh consistently demonstrates strategic thinking abilities, adeptly crafting compelling content, managing advertising campaigns, and fostering online communities. His adeptness in harnessing the power of Amazon ads translates into tangible and impactful results.

TABLE OF CONTENTS

- What is Amazon FBA?
- How Amazon FBA Works
- Pros and Cons of Amazon FBA
- Eligibility and Requirements for FBA
- Account Setup for FBA Sellers
- Creating an FBA Listing
- Sending Inventory to Amazon Fulfillment Centers
- Inventory Storage and Fees
- Monitoring FBA Inventory Levels
- Handling Inventory Removal and Disposal
- Order Processing in FBA
- Returns and Refunds Management
- Handling Lost or Damaged Inventory
- Breakdown of FBA Fees
- Fee Optimization Strategies
- Using Amazon's Partnered Carrier Program
- International Shipping with FBA
- Amazon's Customer Service for FBA Orders
- Managing Customer Feedback and Reviews
- Ensuring FBA Account Health
- Leveraging FBA for Prime Eligibility
- Advertising and Driving Traffic to FBA Products
- Promotions and Deals for FBA Sellers
- Using Multi-Channel Fulfillment (MCF)
- Scaling Your Business with FBA
- FBA for Private Label and Wholesale
- FBA Product Compliance and Safety Requirements
- Analyzing FBA Performance Reports
- Profitability with FBA

What is Amazon FBA?

Fulfillment by Amazon (FBA) is a service that allows sellers to store their products in Amazon's fulfillment centers. When a customer places an order, Amazon handles the picking, packing, shipping, and customer service on behalf of the seller. This enables sellers to leverage Amazon's extensive logistics network and offer benefits like fast, reliable shipping to customers.

By using FBA, sellers can focus more on marketing and growing their business, as Amazon manages the complexities of order fulfillment and customer service. This service is particularly beneficial for those looking to scale their operations without investing heavily in their own warehousing and shipping infrastructure.

However, it's important to note that FBA involves certain fees, including storage and fulfillment costs, which sellers should consider when evaluating its suitability for their business.

How Amazon FBA Works

Fulfillment by Amazon (FBA) is a service that enables sellers to leverage Amazon's extensive logistics network for storing, packing, shipping, and providing customer service for their products. Here's how the FBA process works:

1. **Register for FBA**: If you're already an Amazon seller, you can enroll in FBA through your Seller Central account. New sellers need to create an Amazon selling account and then opt into FBA.
2. **Create Product Listings**: Add your products to the Amazon catalog. You can list new products or convert existing listings to FBA. Ensure that your product details are accurate and comply with Amazon's guidelines.
3. **Prepare and Ship Products to Amazon**: Package your products according to Amazon's packing guidelines to ensure they arrive safely at the fulfillment centers. Use the "Send to Amazon" workflow in Seller Central to create shipments and generate shipping labels. You can choose to ship products as small parcel deliveries or in pallets with less-than-truckload delivery.
4. **Amazon Stores Your Products**: Once received, Amazon stores your products in their fulfillment centers. Your inventory is tracked and managed through your Seller Central account, allowing you to monitor stock levels and manage replenishments.
5. **Customer Orders Your Product**: When a customer places an order for your product, Amazon handles the picking, packing, and shipping of the item. Products

fulfilled through FBA are eligible for Amazon Prime, offering customers fast and reliable shipping options.
6. **Amazon Manages Customer Service and Returns**: Amazon provides customer service for FBA orders, handling inquiries, refunds, and returns. This ensures a consistent experience for customers and reduces the operational burden on sellers.

By utilizing FBA, sellers can focus on growing their business while Amazon manages the complexities of fulfillment and customer service. However, it's important to consider the associated fees, such as storage and fulfillment costs, to ensure that FBA aligns with your business model.

Pros and Cons of Amazon FBA

Pros:

1. **Prime Eligibility**: Products fulfilled by Amazon are eligible for Amazon Prime benefits, including free two-day or same-day shipping. This increases visibility and appeal to millions of Prime members.
2. **Scalability**: FBA simplifies logistics, allowing you to scale your business without worrying about warehousing or shipping logistics.

3. **Customer Trust**: Orders fulfilled by Amazon are often trusted more by customers due to Amazon's strong reputation.
4. **Multi-Channel Fulfillment (MCF)**: You can use FBA to fulfill orders from other sales channels, such as your own website or other marketplaces.
5. **Amazon-Managed Customer Service**: Amazon handles customer inquiries, returns, and refunds, saving you time and effort.
6. **Fast and Reliable Delivery**: Amazon's advanced logistics ensure that your customers receive their orders quickly and reliably.
7. **Increased Buy Box Chances**: FBA listings are often more likely to win the Buy Box, leading to higher conversion rates.
8. **Global Reach**: With Amazon's extensive global infrastructure, you can sell to customers worldwide with minimal setup.

Cons:

1. **Cost**: FBA fees can add up, including storage fees, fulfillment fees, and optional prep service fees. Long-term storage fees can be particularly high if inventory doesn't sell quickly.
2. **Inventory Management**: You need to closely monitor inventory levels to avoid stockouts or overstocking, which can result in additional fees.
3. **Loss of Brand Control**: Since Amazon handles fulfillment and customer service, you have less control

over the customer experience compared to fulfilling orders yourself.
4. **Returns Handling**: Amazon's lenient return policies can lead to higher return rates for FBA sellers. Returned items are sometimes reshelved without proper quality checks.
5. **Commingling Inventory**: Amazon may mix your inventory with other sellers' identical products, risking counterfeit issues or poor-quality items being sent to customers.
6. **Learning Curve**: New sellers may find it challenging to navigate the FBA program's requirements, such as packaging, labeling, and shipping guidelines.
7. **Competition**: FBA levels the playing field, so you'll compete directly with other sellers offering similar products with the same shipping benefits.
8. **Storage Restrictions**: Amazon may impose storage limits based on your account's performance, particularly during peak seasons like Q4.

Amazon FBA can significantly simplify operations and boost sales for many sellers. However, it's crucial to assess your business model, profit margins, and operational needs to determine whether FBA is the right choice.

Eligibility and Requirements for FBA

To participate in FBA, sellers must meet specific eligibility criteria and adhere to certain requirements:

Seller Account Requirements:

- **Amazon Seller Account:** You must have an active Amazon seller account. If you don't have one, you can register on Amazon's Seller Central platform.

Product Eligibility:

- **Permitted Products:** Most products eligible for sale on Amazon can be fulfilled through FBA. However, certain items, such as alcoholic beverages and tires, are prohibited. Additionally, products classified as hazardous materials (hazmat) are typically ineligible for FBA.
- **Expiration-Dated Products:** Items with expiration dates must comply with specific requirements related to shelf life. Ensure these products meet Amazon's guidelines before enrolling them in FBA.

Inventory Preparation and Shipping:

- **Product Labeling:** Each item must have a scannable barcode (UPC, EAN, ISBN, JAN, GTIN, etc.). If a product lacks a physical barcode, it must be labeled accordingly. Amazon offers an FBA Label Service to assist with labeling for a per-unit fee.

- **Packaging Standards:** Products should be prepared and packaged following Amazon's packing guidelines to ensure safe and secure transportation to fulfillment centers. Improperly prepared items may incur additional fees for unplanned services.
- **Shipping Plans:** Sellers must create shipping plans in Seller Central, print shipment ID labels, and send shipments to designated Amazon fulfillment centers. Adhering to Amazon's shipping and routing requirements is essential.

Additional Considerations:

- **Inventory Storage:** Amazon charges storage fees based on the volume of inventory stored in their fulfillment centers. Long-term storage fees apply to items stored for more than 365 days.
- **Fulfillment Fees:** Fees are charged per unit for picking, packing, shipping, handling, customer service, and product returns. These fees vary depending on the product's size and weight.

By meeting these eligibility criteria and adhering to the outlined requirements, sellers can effectively utilize Amazon's FBA program to streamline their fulfillment processes and enhance customer satisfaction.

Account Setup for FBA Sellers

Setting up an Amazon FBA (Fulfillment by Amazon) seller account involves several key steps to ensure a smooth start to your selling journey. Here's a comprehensive guide to help you get started:

1. **Register for an Amazon Seller Account:**

   - **Visit Amazon Seller Central:** Navigate to Amazon Seller Central.
   - **Choose a Selling Plan:** Decide between the **Individual** and **Professional** selling plans. The Individual plan is suitable for those planning to sell fewer than 40 items per month, while the Professional plan is ideal for higher volumes and offers additional features.
   - **Provide Business Information:** You'll need to supply details such as your business name, address, and contact information. If you're operating as an individual, select the appropriate option during registration.
   - **Verify Your Identity:** Amazon requires verification of your identity, which typically takes up to three business days. Ensure you have the necessary documents ready for this process.

2. **Enroll in Fulfillment by Amazon (FBA):**

   - **Access Your Seller Account:** Log in to your Amazon Seller Central account.

- **Navigate to Account Settings:** Click on the gear icon in the top-right corner and select "Account Info."
- **Register for FBA:** Under the "Your Services" section, click on "Manage" and then select "Register for FBA." Follow the prompts to complete the enrollment.

3. Create Product Listings:

- **Add Products to the Catalog:** In Seller Central, go to the "Inventory" tab and select "Add a Product."
- **Provide Product Details:** Enter necessary information such as product title, description, images, and pricing.
- **Specify Fulfillment Method:** For each product, choose "Fulfilled by Amazon" to enroll it in the FBA program.

4. Prepare and Ship Your Products to Amazon:

- **Review Packaging Guidelines:** Ensure your products are packaged according to Amazon's requirements to prevent damage during transit.
- **Label Your Products:** Each item must have a scannable barcode. If your products don't have manufacturer barcodes, you'll need to print and apply Amazon barcodes. Alternatively, you can use Amazon's FBA Label Service for a per-unit fee.
- **Create a Shipping Plan:** In Seller Central, navigate to "Inventory" > "Manage FBA Inventory," select the products you want to ship, and choose "Send/Replenish Inventory." Follow the steps to create a shipping plan, print shipment ID labels, and

send your products to the designated Amazon fulfillment centers.

5. **Monitor Your Inventory and Sales:**

- **Track Inventory Levels:** Regularly check your inventory status in Seller Central to ensure you maintain adequate stock levels.
- **Analyze Sales Performance:** Utilize Amazon's reporting tools to monitor sales trends, customer feedback, and other key metrics to optimize your business strategy.

Creating an FBA Listing

Creating an FBA (Fulfillment by Amazon) listing is an essential step to sell products through Amazon's fulfillment network. Here's a step-by-step guide to help you create an FBA listing effectively:

Step 1: Log in to Seller Central

1. Go to Amazon Seller Central.
2. Enter your credentials to log in.

Step 2: Navigate to Add a Product

1. In the **Inventory** tab, select **Add a Product**.

2. You will have two options:
   Add a product already sold on Amazon: Search by name, ASIN, or UPC if the product exists on Amazon.

   Create a new product listing: If your product is unique, choose this option.

Step 3: Provide Product Information

1. **Product Name**: Enter a clear and concise product title.
2. **Category**: Select the most relevant category for your product.
3. **Brand Name**: Enter your brand name or specify "Generic" if it's not branded.
4. **Product ID**: Enter a UPC, EAN, or GTIN. If you qualify for a GTIN exemption, you can skip this.
5. **Key Product Features**: List the primary features (use bullet points).
6. **Product Description**: Provide a detailed description to highlight the benefits.

Step 4: Add Images

1. Upload high-quality images that meet Amazon's guidelines:
   Main image with a pure white background.
   Product should cover at least 85% of the image.
   Minimum resolution: 1000 x 1000 pixels.
   Use additional slots to showcase your product from multiple angles.

Step 5: Set Pricing

1. Specify the price for your product.
2. Optionally, set a sale price and provide start/end dates for promotions.

Step 6: Select Fulfillment Method

1. When prompted, select **Fulfilled by Amazon (FBA)** as the fulfillment option.
2. Confirm your choice to let Amazon handle storage, packing, and shipping.

Step 7: Submit the Listing

3. Review all the details.
4. Click **Save and Finish** to publish the listing.

Sending Inventory to Amazon Fulfillment Centers

Sending your inventory to Amazon's Fulfillment Centers is a crucial step in utilizing the Fulfillment by Amazon (FBA) service. Follow this step-by-step guide to ensure a smooth process:

1. Prepare Your Products

- **Ensure Compliance:** Verify that your product meet Amazon's FBA product requirements, including packaging and labeling standards.
- **Labeling:** Each item must have a scannable barcode (UPC, EAN, ISBN, or FNSKU). If your products lack these, you'll need to print and apply Amazon barcodes. Alternatively, you can use Amazon's FBA Label Service for a per-unit fee.

2. Create a Shipping Plan

- **Access Seller Central:** Log in to your Amazon Seller Central account.
- **Navigate to Inventory:** Go to the "Inventory" tab and select "Manage FBA Inventory."
- **Select Products:** Choose the products you want to send and click on "Send/Replenish Inventory."
- **Choose Shipping Workflow:** Amazon offers the "Send to Amazon" workflow, which streamlines the shipment creation process.

3. Provide Shipment Details

- **Ship-From Address:** Enter the address from which you're shipping the products.
- **Packing Details:** Specify whether the shipment contains individual products or case-packed products.
- **Quantity:** Indicate the number of units per product.

4. Prepare Shipment

- **Packing:** Pack your products according to Amazon's packaging guidelines to prevent damage during transit.
- **Box Content Information:** Provide details about the contents of each box, including quantities and weights.

5. Label and Ship

- **Print Labels:** Print the FBA shipment labels provided by Amazon. Ensure each box has its own label, placed next to the carrier label.
- **Choose Carrier:** Select a carrier for shipping. Amazon's Partnered Carrier Program offers discounted rates.
- **Ship the Products:** Send your labeled boxes to the designated Amazon Fulfillment Centers.

6. Monitor Shipment Status

- **Track Shipment:** Use the tracking information provided by your carrier to monitor the shipment's progress.
- **Confirm Receipt:** Once Amazon receives and processes your shipment, your inventory will be available for sale.

By following these steps, you can efficiently send your inventory to Amazon's Fulfillment Centers, ensuring your products are ready for customers promptly.

Inventory Storage and Fees

Amazon's Fulfillment by Amazon (FBA) program offers sellers the convenience of storing products in Amazon's fulfillment centers, where Amazon handles storage, packaging, shipping, and customer service. However, this service incurs specific fees that sellers should understand to manage costs effectively.

1. Monthly Inventory Storage Fees:

Amazon charges monthly fees based on the volume of inventory stored in their fulfillment centers. These fees are calculated per cubic foot and vary depending on the product size and the time of year:

- **Standard-Size Products:**
  January – September: $0.75 per cubic foot.
  October – December: $2.40 per cubic foot.
- **Oversize Products:**
  January – September: $0.48 per cubic foot.
  October – December: $1.20 per cubic foot.

The higher rates during the fourth quarter (October to December) reflect increased demand for storage space during the holiday season.

2. Aged Inventory Surcharge (formerly Long-Term Storage Fees):

To encourage efficient inventory management, Amazon imposes surcharges on items stored for extended periods:

- **Inventory aged 181 to 210 days:** $0.50 per cubic foot.
- **Inventory aged 211 to 240 days:** $1.00 per cubic foot.
- **Inventory aged 241 to 270 days:** $1.50 per cubic foot.
- **Inventory aged 271 to 300 days:** $2.00 per cubic foot.
- **Inventory aged 301 to 330 days:** $2.50 per cubic foot.
- **Inventory aged 331 to 365 days:** $3.00 per cubic foot.
- **Inventory aged over 365 days:** $6.90 per cubic foot or $0.15 per unit, whichever is greater.

These surcharges are assessed monthly and are in addition to the standard monthly storage fees.

3. Removal and Disposal Fees:

If you choose to remove or dispose of inventory from Amazon's fulfillment centers, the following fees apply:

- **Standard-Size Items:**
  Removal Fee: $0.97 per unit.
  Disposal Fee: $0.97 per unit.

- **Oversize Items:**
  Removal Fee: $1.34 per unit.
  Disposal Fee: $1.34 per unit.

These fees cover the cost of returning items to you or disposing of them on your behalf.

4. Unplanned Service Fees:

If your inventory arrives at the fulfillment center without proper preparation or labeling, Amazon may perform these services for you and charge unplanned service fees. To avoid these additional costs, ensure your products comply with Amazon's packaging and labeling requirements before shipment.

5. FBA Fulfillment Fees:

In addition to storage fees, Amazon charges fulfillment fees for picking, packing, shipping, and handling customer service for your orders. These fees are based on the product's size and weight.

Best Practices to Manage FBA Fees:

- **Monitor Inventory Age:** Regularly review your inventory age to identify slow-moving items and take action before surcharges apply.
- **Optimize Stock Levels:** Maintain optimal inventory levels to balance storage costs with product availability.
- **Utilize Removal Orders:** For slow-moving or seasonal items, consider creating removal orders to avoid long-term storage fees.

By understanding and actively managing these fees, you can optimize your profitability while leveraging Amazon's fulfillment services.

Monitoring FBA Inventory Levels

Monitoring your FBA inventory levels is essential to avoid stockouts, minimize storage fees, and optimize sales. Amazon provides various tools and reports to help sellers manage their inventory effectively. Here's a step-by-step guide:

1. Use Amazon Seller Central Inventory Dashboard

- **Navigate to the Dashboard**:
  Log in to **Seller Central**.
  Go to the **Inventory** tab and select **Manage FBA Inventory**.
- **Key Features**:
  Restock Alerts: Amazon provides recommendations on when to restock based on sales velocity.
  Excess Inventory Alerts: Helps identify overstocked items that may incur higher storage fees.

2. Set Up Automated Inventory Alerts

- Go to **Settings** > **Notifications**.

1. **Understanding Removal and Disposal Orders**

    - **Removal Orders**: Request to have your inventory returned to you or a designated address. This is suitable for items you wish to sell through other channels or inspect for quality issues.
    - **Disposal Orders**: Authorize Amazon to dispose of your inventory. This is appropriate for items that are unsellable or not worth the cost of return shipping.

2. **Initiating a Removal or Disposal Order**

    - **Access Seller Central**:

        Log in to your Amazon Seller Central account.

    - **Navigate to Inventory**:

        Go to the **Inventory** tab and select **Manage FBA Inventory**.

    - **Select Items**:

        Check the boxes next to the items you want to remove or dispose of.

    - **Create Removal Order**:

        From the **Action on Selected** drop-down menu, choose **Create removal order**.

    - **Specify Details**:

Method of Removal: Select either **Return to Address** or **Dispose**.

Return Address: If returning, provide the address where you want the items sent.
Quantity: Indicate the number of units for removal or disposal.

- **Review and Confirm**:

    Review the order details, including estimated fees, and confirm the removal or disposal order.

3. Fees Associated with Removal and Disposal

Amazon charges fees for both removal and disposal orders, which vary based on the size and weight of the items:

- **Standard-Size Items**:
  Removal Fee: $0.97 per unit.
  Disposal Fee: $0.97 per unit.
- **Oversize Items**:
  Removal Fee: $1.34 per unit.
  Disposal Fee: $1.34 per unit.

These fees cover the cost of returning items to you or disposing of them on your behalf.

4. Monitoring Removal and Disposal Orders

- **Track Orders**:
  In Seller Central, navigate to **Inventory** > **Manage FBA**

Shipments > **Removal Order Detail** to monitor the status of your removal or disposal orders.
- **Processing Time**:
  Removal and disposal orders typically take 10-14 business days to process, but times may vary.

5. Best Practices

- **Regular Inventory Audits**:
  Periodically review your inventory to identify slow-moving or unsellable items.
- **Cost-Benefit Analysis**:
  Compare the costs of removal versus disposal to determine the most economical option.
- **Automated Removals**:
  Set up automated removal orders for aged inventory to avoid long-term storage fees.

By proactively managing your FBA inventory through removal and disposal orders, you can reduce unnecessary storage fees and maintain a streamlined inventory that aligns with your sales strategy.

Order Processing in FBA

Fulfillment by Amazon (FBA) streamlines the order processing workflow for sellers by managing key fulfillment tasks. Here's an overview of how FBA handles order processing:

1. Customer Places an Order

- A customer purchases a product listed by an FBA seller on Amazon's marketplace.

2. Order Notification

- Amazon's system automatically records the order and notifies the appropriate fulfillment center where the seller's inventory is stored.

3. Picking the Product

- Warehouse staff locate the ordered item within the fulfillment center.

4. Packing the Product

- The item is securely packed using appropriate materials to ensure it reaches the customer in good condition.

5. Shipping the Product

- Amazon ships the package to the customer using its logistics network, providing tracking information for both the seller and the customer.

6. Handling Customer Service and Returns

- Amazon manages customer inquiries related to the order and processes returns or refunds as needed.

By leveraging FBA, sellers can focus on other aspects of their business while Amazon handles the complexities of order fulfillment.

Returns and Refunds Management

Managing returns and refunds effectively is essential to maintaining customer satisfaction and optimizing your business operations on Amazon. Here's a breakdown of how returns and refunds are managed in Amazon FBA:

1. Return Policy for FBA Sellers

- **Amazon's Return Window**: For most products, Amazon offers a 30-day return policy, but some categories may have different terms.
- **Refunds**: If a customer returns a product within the return window, Amazon processes the refund, including shipping fees (if applicable), directly to the customer.

2. Return Requests

- **Customer Initiates a Return:**
  The customer requests a return via their Amazon account.
  Amazon provides a return shipping label (if applicable), and the customer ships the product back to an Amazon fulfillment center.
- **Return Eligibility:**
  Items that are undamaged, in original packaging, and in resellable condition typically qualify for return. Some items may not be eligible for return, such as perishable goods or items with specific restrictions.

3. Processing Returns at the Fulfillment Center

- **Receiving the Return:** Once the return package arrives at the Amazon fulfillment center, Amazon inspects the item.
- **Condition Check:** If the product is in a sellable condition, it will be restocked. Otherwise, it may be marked as unsellable and sent back to the seller (if requested).

4. Refunds to the Customer

- **Amazon's Role:** Once Amazon receives the returned item and processes it, they initiate a refund to the customer. The refund typically includes:
  - The purchase price of the item.
  - Any applicable taxes.
  - Shipping costs, depending on the reason for return.

5. Refunds to Sellers

- **Refund Process**: Sellers are generally not required to refund the customer directly; Amazon manages this. However, the amount is deducted from the seller's account balance.
- **Restocking Fees**: If a customer returns a product due to buyer's remorse, Amazon may charge a restocking fee (typically 20% of the item price) to cover the cost of handling the return.
- **Return on Refund (A-Z Guarantee)**: If a customer files a claim under Amazon's A-Z Guarantee, Amazon may issue a refund without the seller's consent, based on the customer's complaint.

6. Manage Return Requests and Refunds in Seller Central

- **Viewing Returns**: Sellers can track and manage returns by going to **Orders** > **Manage Returns** in Seller Central. This allows sellers to see the status of returns and decide whether to appeal return requests in certain cases.
- **Appealing Returns**: Sellers can dispute a return if they believe the customer has abused the return policy, or if the item is not damaged. The process includes submitting evidence to Amazon's Seller Performance team.

7. Returns and Refunds Fees

- **Restocking Fees**: As mentioned earlier, Amazon may charge a restocking fee for non-defective returns.

- **Return Processing Fees**: FBA sellers are charged a **Return Processing Fee** for each returned item. This fee varies by product category but is typically lower than the standard FBA fees.

8. Best Practices for Handling Returns and Refunds

- **Quality Control**: Ensure your products are high-quality and meet customer expectations to minimize returns.
- **Clear Product Listings**: Provide accurate and detailed product descriptions to reduce misunderstandings that could lead to returns.
- **Customer Service**: Be responsive to customer inquiries about returns and refunds to build trust.
- **Monitor Return Rates**: Regularly review your return rate metrics in Seller Central to identify any issues with specific products or categories.

9. Managing Aged or Unsellable Returns

- **Removal Orders**: Sellers can create removal orders for unsellable or defective returns. These items can either be returned to you or disposed of by Amazon, depending on your preference.
- **Disposal Fees**: There are fees associated with the disposal of unsellable returns, so it's essential to decide whether returning or disposing of these products is more cost-effective.

By effectively managing returns and refunds, you can maintain a positive customer experience while keeping costs under control. Monitoring your return rate and responding promptly to any issues that arise is key to success with Amazon FBA.

Handling Lost or Damaged Inventory

Handling lost or damaged inventory is a critical aspect of managing an FBA business on Amazon. When inventory is lost, damaged, or otherwise compromised in Amazon's fulfillment network, it can impact your revenue and overall seller health. Here's a step-by-step guide on how to address these issues:

1. Reporting Lost or Damaged Inventory

Amazon takes responsibility for lost or damaged items that occur while they are in their fulfillment centers. If inventory is damaged or lost, Amazon will typically notify you via the **FBA Inventory Adjustments** report.

- **Steps to Access the Report:**
  - Go to **Reports** > **Fulfillment** > **Inventory Adjustments**.
  - This report will list any discrepancies in your inventory, including damaged or lost goods.

Amazon also has an **FBA Lost and Damaged Inventory Claims Process** that allows sellers to request reimbursement if the inventory is lost or damaged while stored at an Amazon warehouse.

2. FBA Reimbursement for Lost or Damaged Inventory

Amazon will reimburse sellers for lost or damaged inventory that occurs within their fulfillment centers, but the process may take some time.

- **How to File a Claim**:
  - **Automatically**: In many cases, Amazon will automatically initiate reimbursement once the system identifies lost or damaged inventory. This usually happens after 30 days, but it can vary depending on the situation.
  - **Manually**: If you don't see a reimbursement for lost or damaged items, you can file a claim:
    - Navigate to **Seller Central**.
    - Go to **Help** > **Get Support** > **FBA Inventory Issues** > **Lost or Damaged Inventory**.
    - Follow the prompts to file a claim.
- **Reimbursement Process**:
  - If approved, Amazon will reimburse you based on the **current selling price** of the lost or damaged inventory, excluding any shipping fees.
  - The reimbursement is credited to your seller account balance.
- **Reimbursement Criteria**:
  - Inventory lost or damaged at an Amazon fulfillment center will be eligible for reimbursement.

- Sellers need to have proper documentation (such as the FBA Inventory Adjustments report) to support their claims.

3. Investigating Causes of Loss or Damage

If you notice frequent issues with lost or damaged inventory, consider investigating the following causes:

- **Fulfillment Center Handling**:
  - Occasionally, Amazon's fulfillment centers might mishandle items. Monitoring reports and consistently checking inventory can help identify patterns that may require further action.
- **Inaccurate Shipments**:
  - Sometimes, sellers report inventory as shipped when it hasn't been sent correctly. Double-check your shipments to ensure you've fulfilled orders properly.
- **Improper Packaging**:
  - Make sure your products are packaged securely to avoid damage during Amazon's handling and shipping process.

4. Preventive Measures to Avoid Future Issues

While you can't completely eliminate the possibility of lost or damaged inventory, you can take steps to minimize the risk:

- **Track Inventory**:
  - Regularly monitor your inventory levels in **Seller Central** using the **FBA Inventory Management** tool.

Stay updated on any discrepancies or unusual changes in inventory levels.
- **Proper Packaging:**
  - Ensure your items are packaged properly to prevent damage during handling. Follow Amazon's **FBA packaging requirements** to reduce the risk of damaged goods.
- **Shipping Accuracy:**
  - Confirm that all shipments are correctly labeled and contain the right quantities. Use **Amazon's shipment creation workflow** to reduce the chances of errors in shipments.
- **Use Quality Control:**
  - Perform regular checks on your products before sending them to Amazon's fulfillment centers to ensure they are in good condition.
- **Report Damages Immediately:**
  - If you receive products that are damaged during shipping to Amazon's fulfillment center, file a report immediately to ensure the issue is addressed quickly.

5. Handling Damaged Returns

If a customer returns a damaged product, you have two options:

- **Inspection**: If the item is returned to you, inspect it to determine if it's still resellable. If it is, you can restock it; if not, you can file a removal request to have it returned or disposed of.

- **Reimbursement for Returns**: If the item is returned as damaged by the customer, you may be eligible for reimbursement through Amazon's **A-to-Z Guarantee** if the return was due to a fulfillment error.

6. FBA Insurance Options

Although Amazon covers some types of lost or damaged inventory, it's a good idea to consider additional protection, especially for high-value items. Some sellers choose to purchase **third-party insurance** for extra coverage on their inventory stored in Amazon's warehouses.

7. Disputing Reimbursements (If Necessary)

If you believe Amazon has made an error in handling your reimbursement claim, you can dispute it:

- **Review the FBA Inventory Adjustments Report**: Compare the report with your own records to check for discrepancies.
- **Submit Documentation**: Provide supporting documentation if you believe an error has occurred. This could include shipment tracking information or inventory receipts.

To dispute a reimbursement, contact Amazon Seller Support under **Help > Get Support > FBA Inventory Issues > Dispute Reimbursement**.

8. Key Takeaways

- **Monitor Inventory Levels**: Regularly check your inventory adjustments report to catch any discrepancies early.
- **File Claims Promptly**: If your inventory is lost or damaged in Amazon's fulfillment centers, file a claim to receive reimbursement.
- **Prevention**: Improve packaging, shipment accuracy, and inventory tracking to minimize future issues.

Handling lost or damaged inventory efficiently helps maintain your cash flow and ensures customer satisfaction, while minimizing the impact of these occurrences on your FBA business.

Breakdown of FBA Fees

FBA fees can vary depending on the size, weight, and category of the products you're selling. Amazon charges fees to cover the cost of storing, picking, packing, and shipping your products from their fulfillment centers. Here's a breakdown of the key FBA fees you should be aware of:

1. Fulfillment Fees

Fulfillment fees cover the cost of storing, picking, packing, and shipping your inventory. These fees are based on the size and weight of the product.

- **Standard-Size Items**: These are smaller and lighter items (up to 2 lb, typically).

Weight Range Fee per Unit (as of 2024)

Weight Range	Fee
Up to 4 oz	$2.50
4 oz to 8 oz	$3.31
8 oz to 1 lb	$3.83
1 lb to 2 lb	$5.11

- **Oversize Items**: These are larger or heavier items (over 2 lb or larger than 18" x 14" x 8" dimensions).

Size Category	Fee per Unit (as of 2024)
Small Oversize	$8.26
Medium Oversize	$10.72
Large Oversize	$12.57
Special Oversize	$15.75

2. Monthly Storage Fees

Amazon charges monthly storage fees to store your inventory in their fulfillment centers. These fees depend on the time of year and the volume of inventory you have.

- **Standard-Size Items**:
  - January - September: **$0.75 per cubic foot**
  - October - December: **$2.40 per cubic foot** (higher due to increased holiday storage demand)
- **Oversize Items**:
  - January - September: **$0.48 per cubic foot**
  - October - December: **$1.20 per cubic foot**

3. Long-Term Storage Fees

If inventory stays in Amazon's warehouses for more than 365 days, it may be subject to long-term storage fees.

- **Long-Term Storage Fee**:
  - **$6.90 per cubic foot** or **$15 per unit**, whichever is greater.
  - These fees are assessed twice a year (in February and August), so it's important to manage your inventory to avoid overstocking and unsellable items.

4. Removal Fees

If you want to remove unsellable or excess inventory from Amazon's fulfillment centers, Amazon charges a removal fee.

- **Standard-Size Items: $0.97 per unit.**

- **Oversize Items**: $1.34 per unit.

These items can be returned to you or disposed of.

5. Return Processing Fees

When a customer returns a product, Amazon charges a return processing fee for FBA orders, which varies depending on the product category.

- **Standard-Size Items**: Typically $2.00 - $5.00, depending on the weight.
- **Oversize Items**: Higher fees, usually based on the size and weight of the item.

6. Labeling Fees

If you choose to have Amazon label your products for you (instead of labeling them yourself), Amazon will charge a labeling fee.

- **Labeling Fee**: $0.30 per unit.

This is only applicable if your products need unique labeling, and you choose to use Amazon's labeling service.

7. Removal and Disposal Fees

If you request Amazon to dispose of your unsellable products instead of returning them, a disposal fee will apply.

- **Standard-Size Items**: $0.15 per unit.

- **Oversize Items**: $0.30 per unit.

8. Amazon FBA Multichannel Fulfillment Fees

If you use FBA to fulfill orders from other sales channels (such as your website or other platforms), Amazon charges additional fees for shipping these orders.

- Fees are similar to regular FBA fulfillment fees but can vary depending on the shipping destination and product size.

9. FBA New Selection Program Fees

If you're a new seller or new to FBA, Amazon offers a program to help reduce storage and fulfillment fees for new-to-FBA products.

- **Program Benefits**:
  - Lower storage fees for the first 180 days.
  - Reduced fulfillment fees for products that are new to FBA.

10. Advertising Costs

While not part of the core FBA fees, if you're using **Amazon PPC** (Pay-Per-Click) ads to drive traffic to your FBA products, you'll incur advertising costs based on how much you bid for your keywords and your overall ad strategy.

Summary of Key FBA Fees

Fee Type	Standard Size (Up to 1 lb)	Oversize (Large Item)
Fulfillment Fee	$2.50 - $5.11	$8.26 - $15.75
Storage Fee (Monthly)	$0.75 per cubic foot	$0.48 per cubic foot
Long-Term Storage Fee	$6.90 per cubic foot	$6.90 per cubic foot
Removal Fee	$0.97 per unit	$1.34 per unit
Return Processing Fee	$2.00 - $5.00	Higher for large items
Labeling Fee	$0.30 per unit	$0.30 per unit
Disposal Fee	$0.15 per unit	$0.30 per unit

Tips to Minimize FBA Fees

1. **Monitor Inventory Health**: Avoid long-term storage fees by regularly removing or discounting slow-moving inventory.
2. **Use Amazon's FBA Calculator**: This tool helps you calculate the impact of FBA fees on profitability.
3. **Optimize Packaging**: Lighter, smaller packaging reduces both storage and fulfillment fees.

4. **Plan Inventory Levels**: Keep track of seasonal fluctuations to avoid overstocking and excessive storage fees during peak times.

By understanding and effectively managing these FBA fees, you can better plan your pricing, inventory management, and profit margins.

Fee Optimization Strategies

Fee optimization is an essential aspect of running a profitable business on Amazon FBA. By minimizing costs, you can significantly improve your bottom line. Here are several strategies to help optimize your FBA fees:

1. Optimize Product Sizing and Weight

The size and weight of your products directly affect your FBA fulfillment fees, storage fees, and long-term storage fees. Here's how to optimize:

- **Use the smallest possible packaging**: Minimize the size of your packaging to reduce both storage and fulfillment fees. For instance, if your product can fit into a smaller box, use it to avoid oversized fees.
- **Keep product weight under 2 lbs**: Products that weigh less than 2 lbs tend to have lower fulfillment fees.

Consider sourcing lighter alternatives or adjusting packaging to reduce weight.
- **Avoid oversized inventory**: Oversize items incur much higher storage and fulfillment fees. If possible, modify your products to fit into standard size categories.

2. Utilize Amazon's FBA Calculator

The **FBA Revenue Calculator** is a tool provided by Amazon that helps you estimate the costs and fees for different products based on their size, weight, and category. Use it to assess profitability and adjust your pricing strategy accordingly.

- **Review Fulfillment Fees**: Check how different dimensions and weights impact fulfillment costs.
- **Compare Costs Across Multiple Listings**: Compare different product options, including smaller or lighter versions, to see which ones offer a better fee structure.

3. Inventory Management and Storage Optimization

Storage fees can add up quickly, especially during peak seasons. Here's how to manage your inventory more effectively:

- **Use Amazon's FBA Inventory Performance Index (IPI)**: Monitor your IPI to avoid high storage fees. A low IPI can result in inventory limits or increased fees. To maintain a high IPI:
  - **Reduce Excess Inventory**: If you have products that

are not selling well, remove or discount them to avoid long-term storage fees.
- **Implement Just-In-Time Inventory**: Keep enough stock to meet demand without overstocking. This can help you avoid excess storage fees.
- **Take Advantage of Seasonal Storage Discounts**: If your product is seasonal (e.g., holiday-related), ensure that you plan your inventory to avoid high storage fees during Amazon's peak seasons (October–December).
- **Use Amazon's Multi-Channel Fulfillment (MCF)**: If you sell on other platforms or your website, use FBA to fulfill orders from those channels as well, leveraging the same storage capacity and fee structure.

4. Optimize Your Removal Strategy

If your products are slow-moving or have excess inventory in Amazon's warehouses, consider using the **removal service** to return or dispose of unsellable items.

- **Regularly Monitor Inventory Health**: Use **Inventory Health Reports** to track aging inventory and decide which items need to be removed or liquidated.
- **Remove Damaged Goods**: Any damaged products should be removed as soon as possible to avoid paying for storage and fulfillment of unsellable goods.

5. Choose the Right Labeling and Prep Option

Amazon allows sellers to either label and prep their products themselves or use Amazon's prep services for a fee. Choosing the best option can help you reduce unnecessary costs:

- **Label Your Products**: If you have a small number of SKUs and the ability to label them in bulk, doing this yourself can save $0.30 per unit.
- **Evaluate Prep Fees**: Amazon charges a fee for prepping your inventory (e.g., bagging, bubble wrapping). If your products require special preparation (e.g., fragile items), evaluate if doing it yourself or outsourcing it is cheaper.

6. Minimize Long-Term Storage Fees

Long-term storage fees are charged on inventory that has been in Amazon's fulfillment centers for over 365 days. To avoid these fees:

- **Monitor Your Inventory Turnover**: Use the **Restock Inventory Report** to track your products' sales velocity. Slow-moving products should be removed or discounted to prevent long-term storage fees.
- **Perform Regular Stock Audits**: Regularly review your inventory to ensure you're not holding onto products that no longer sell well or are becoming obsolete.
- **Use the Amazon FBA Inventory Health Report**: This report helps you track the age of your inventory and plan accordingly.

7. Leverage Amazon's New Selection Program

Amazon's **New Selection Program** offers a discount on storage fees for new-to-FBA products.

- **Take Advantage of Initial Storage Fee Discounts**: If you're launching new products, enroll in this program to reduce your storage costs for the first 180 days.
- **Monitor Your Listings for Eligibility**: Ensure that your products meet the program's criteria to receive the discount.

8. Use Amazon's Small and Light Program

If you're selling lightweight, low-cost items, consider enrolling in the **FBA Small and Light Program**. This program offers reduced fulfillment fees for small and lightweight items (typically under $7 and weighing up to 3 lbs).

- **Eligibility**: Products must be priced below a certain threshold and meet the size and weight criteria.
- **Benefits**: Reduced fulfillment fees, which can help increase your profitability on lower-cost products.

9. Adjust Your Pricing to Account for Fees

To maintain profitability, always factor in FBA fees when setting your product prices. Use Amazon's **Fee Preview Tool** to review how your price adjustments will impact your total FBA fees.

- **Increase Product Price**: If FBA fees increase, consider adjusting your price slightly (without losing competitiveness) to absorb these additional costs.
- **Offer Bundles**: Consider offering product bundles to increase the average order value, which can help you spread your FBA fees across multiple units.

10. Negotiate with Amazon for Discounts

If you're a high-volume seller, Amazon may offer discounts or reduced fees for fulfillment, storage, or long-term storage. Though this is generally available to top-tier sellers, it's worth asking Amazon Seller Support about any special programs that may apply to your business.

Summary of FBA Fee Optimization Strategies

1. **Optimize product size and weight** to reduce fulfillment and storage fees.
2. **Use the FBA Calculator** to evaluate profitability before listing products.
3. **Manage inventory efficiently** by reducing excess stock and avoiding long-term storage fees.
4. **Remove unsellable or excess inventory** to avoid unnecessary storage fees.
5. **Label products yourself** to avoid labeling fees.
6. **Enlist in Amazon's Small and Light Program** for cost-effective fulfillment of lightweight products.
7. **Monitor and adjust pricing** regularly to account for any changes in FBA fees.

8. **Take advantage of Amazon's New Selection Program** to reduce initial storage fees for new products.
9. **Regularly audit inventory** to avoid long-term storage fees.

By carefully monitoring your inventory and FBA fee structure, you can optimize your operations and maintain a profitable business.

Using Amazon's Partnered Carrier Program

Amazon's **Partnered Carrier Program** allows sellers to use Amazon's discounted shipping rates for sending products to fulfillment centers and shipping orders to customers. By leveraging Amazon's agreements with various carriers, sellers can benefit from reduced shipping costs while enjoying the convenience of using a trusted network. Here's an overview of how the **Partnered Carrier Program** works and how you can use it effectively.

1. What Is Amazon's Partnered Carrier Program?

Amazon's Partnered Carrier Program enables sellers to ship their inventory to Amazon fulfillment centers (FBA) and fulfill customer orders using a network of carriers at discounted rates. The program includes both **FBA shipments** (shipping inventory to Amazon's warehouses) and **FBM shipments** (shipping products directly to customers for Merchant Fulfilled Network sellers).

2. Benefits of Using Amazon's Partnered Carrier Program

- **Discounted Shipping Rates**: Amazon partners with carriers like UPS, DHL, and others to offer discounted shipping rates, often lower than what a seller might get on their own.
- **Convenience**: The program integrates with Amazon Seller Central, allowing you to book shipments directly from within your seller account. This streamlines the shipping process and saves time.
- **Tracking Integration**: Shipments made through the Partnered Carrier Program are automatically integrated with Amazon's tracking system, so both you and your customers can track shipments in real-time.
- **No Need for Negotiating Rates**: Since Amazon has negotiated rates with the carriers, you don't need to spend time comparing shipping rates or contacting carriers directly to negotiate discounts.

3. How to Use the Partnered Carrier Program for FBA Shipments

For FBA shipments, you'll use the Partnered Carrier Program to send your products to Amazon fulfillment centers. Here's how to set it up:

A. Setting up Partnered Carrier Program for FBA

1. **Create a Shipment Plan:**
   - Go to **Seller Central > Inventory > Manage FBA Shipments**.
   - Click on **Create a Shipment Plan** and follow the prompts to prepare your inventory for shipment to Amazon's fulfillment center.
2. **Select Partnered Carrier:**
   - Once you've set up your shipment plan, Amazon will offer a list of **Partnered Carriers** to choose from, including UPS and other carriers depending on your location.
   - Amazon will automatically offer discounted rates for eligible shipments based on the size, weight, and destination of your products.
3. **Choose Your Shipping Method:**
   - Amazon will suggest shipping options (e.g., **Standard Ground, Two-Day Delivery**) based on the size of your shipment and the fulfillment center's location.
   - You can select the shipping method that best fits your needs.
4. **Print Shipping Labels:**
   - Once you've selected your carrier and shipping method, you can print shipping labels directly from **Seller Central**.
   - These labels will include everything needed for the shipment, including the destination fulfillment center and any necessary tracking information.
5. **Ship Your Inventory:**
   - Drop off your shipment at the carrier's location (e.g.,

UPS store or authorized drop-off center), or schedule a pickup if available.
- The tracking information will be automatically linked to your shipment, allowing you to track progress in Seller Central.

- **Shipping Fees**: Amazon's partnered carrier rates are typically lower than those you'd pay through standard retail channels.
- **Multiple Carrier Options**: Depending on the region, you may be able to choose from different partnered carriers, like UPS, DHL, or others.
- **Pick-Up Options**: In some regions, Amazon offers a pick-up service for FBA shipments at no extra cost, making it even more convenient for sellers.

4. How to Use the Partnered Carrier Program for FBM Shipments

For **Merchant Fulfilled Network (FBM)** sellers who fulfill orders themselves, Amazon's Partnered Carrier Program can be used to ship customer orders directly from your location to the customer.

1. **Create a Shipment**:
   - Go to **Manage Orders** > **Manage Shipping Settings** in **Seller Central**.
   - Under **Shipping Settings**, you'll be able to choose **Partnered Carrier** options for the shipping services you want to use for your FBM orders.

2. **Choose a Carrier and Service**:
   - You'll have the option to choose from Amazon's partnered carriers, including UPS, depending on your location. You can also select specific service levels (e.g., **Standard Ground, 2-Day Shipping**).

- **Print Labels**:
  - Once you select the carrier and service, you can print shipping labels directly from **Seller Central**.
  - These labels will include tracking numbers and ensure that your FBM order is automatically updated with tracking information in Amazon's system.

  Ship the Product:
  - Drop the package off at the carrier's location or schedule a pickup if available. The tracking number will be automatically linked to the order in **Seller Central**.

  Discounted Shipping Rates: You benefit from Amazon's negotiated rates with carriers.
- **Tracking Integration**: Amazon automatically updates order tracking for both you and the customer, ensuring a seamless experience.
- **Shipping Flexibility**: You can ship directly from your warehouse or home, using Amazon's shipping rate discounts for both domestic and international shipments.

5. Cost of Partnered Carrier Services

The cost of shipping through Amazon's Partnered Carrier Program varies depending on the weight, size, and destination of the shipment, as well as the service level you select. Here's what to expect:

- **Discounted Rates**: Amazon negotiates rates with carriers, so you typically get discounted shipping costs compared to standard retail rates.
- **Shipping Methods**: The program offers various shipping methods including ground, expedited, and international shipping. Rates will differ depending on the method.
- **No Extra Fees for Labeling**: You don't have to pay extra for printing shipping labels through Seller Central.

6. Things to Consider

- **Restricted Locations**: The Partnered Carrier Program may not be available in all countries or regions. Check Amazon's guidelines for details about the countries and regions eligible for the program.
- **Carrier Limitations**: Some shipping carriers may not be available for certain product categories (e.g., hazardous materials). Ensure your products comply with shipping regulations.
- **Shipping Times**: Make sure to check estimated shipping times to avoid delays, especially during peak seasons like holidays.

7. Best Practices for Using Amazon's Partnered Carrier Program

- **Plan Shipments Early**: Avoid last-minute shipping by planning your shipments well in advance, especially during peak seasons when shipping times may increase.
- **Use Amazon's Tracking**: Always check shipment status in **Seller Central** to ensure your inventory is processed on time.
- **Combine Shipments**: If possible, consolidate shipments to reduce overall shipping costs. Amazon offers better rates when you ship larger quantities.
- **Monitor Shipping Costs**: Regularly review the shipping rates for different carriers and service levels to ensure you're using the most cost-effective options.

The **Partnered Carrier Program** offers Amazon sellers discounted shipping rates for both **FBA** and **FBM** shipments, providing ease of use, integrated tracking, and cost savings. Key benefits include discounted rates, simplified logistics, and the convenience of using Amazon's shipping partners, like UPS. Whether shipping inventory to FBA centers or fulfilling customer orders, this program streamlines your shipping processes and helps reduce costs.

International Shipping with FBA

International Shipping with Amazon FBA allows sellers to expand their reach beyond their home country by shipping products to Amazon fulfillment centers in different regions. This gives sellers access to Amazon's global marketplace and helps fulfill international orders efficiently using Amazon's FBA network. Here's how you can use **Amazon FBA's international shipping** services effectively:

1. Key Features of FBA International Shipping

- **Global Reach**: By using FBA, you can store inventory in multiple countries and regions, enabling you to sell to customers in those locations. This gives you access to Amazon's global marketplace, including countries in North America, Europe, and Asia.
- **Simplified Logistics**: FBA handles the storage, packaging, shipping, and customer service for international orders. Once your products are in Amazon's fulfillment centers, Amazon will manage the order fulfillment for you, even if the customer is in another country.
- **Multi-Channel Fulfillment (MCF)**: You can use Amazon's FBA program to fulfill orders on other marketplaces or your own website, not just on Amazon.
- **Amazon Global Selling**: This program allows you to list and sell your products in different countries while keeping all your inventory in one place (if using Fulfillment by Amazon).

2. Setting up FBA for International Sales

To sell internationally with FBA, you need to set up the right configuration and make sure your products are eligible for global selling.

- **Register for Global Selling**: You can sell your products on Amazon marketplaces outside your home country. For example, if you're in the U.S., you can sell on Amazon's marketplaces in the UK, Germany, Japan, and other regions.
- **Choose Target Markets**: Amazon has marketplaces in North America (US, Canada, Mexico), Europe (UK, Germany, France, Spain, Italy, etc.), and Asia (Japan, India, etc.). You can choose which regions you want to target.
- **Multilingual Listings**: Amazon provides translation services to help create listings in the local languages of your target marketplaces.

1. **Create Listings for Each Marketplace**:
   - List your products on the relevant international Amazon marketplace(s).
   - You may need to adjust pricing, images, and descriptions based on the regional preferences of the customers.
2. **Ship Inventory to FBA Fulfillment Centers in Different Countries**:
   - You can use Amazon's **FBA Export** program to ship products to FBA warehouses in your target country. Amazon will guide you on where to

send inventory based on the location of the customers you want to target.
- You'll need to ensure that your products comply with the import/export regulations of the destination country.

3. **FBA Multi-Channel Fulfillment (MCF)**:
   - If you want to sell across multiple marketplaces, you can take advantage of **FBA Multi-Channel Fulfillment** to ship from Amazon's fulfillment centers to other platforms, such as your own website, Shopify store, etc.

4. **Set Up International Shipping Settings**:
   - In **Seller Central**, go to the **Shipping Settings** and specify international shipping preferences for your listings. You can decide which countries you want to ship to and enable international shipping for those locations.

- **Customs and Duties**: When shipping internationally, customs duties and taxes may apply. Amazon automatically collects VAT (Value Added Tax) in countries where applicable, but you should ensure your products comply with local import regulations.
- **Product Compliance**: Ensure your products meet the compliance standards for the target countries. This may involve labeling, certifications, and packaging that comply with local laws.
- **FBA Export**: Amazon's FBA Export service allows you to automatically ship eligible products internationally, and Amazon handles customs and duties for you.

3. Shipping Methods and Costs for International Shipments

When shipping internationally using FBA, you have several options for how your products can be delivered to Amazon fulfillment centers:

1. **FBA Export**: This service is ideal for shipping directly from your home country to international Amazon fulfillment centers.
    - **Benefits**: Amazon provides discounted shipping rates, handles customs paperwork, and takes care of the logistics.
    - **Availability**: FBA Export is available in several countries, but the program may not be available for all sellers or in all regions.
2. **Partnered Carrier Program**: You can use Amazon's **Partnered Carrier Program** for international shipments to FBA centers. Amazon's negotiated rates with carriers like UPS can help you save on international shipping.
    - **International Pickup and Delivery**: Partnered carriers offer international shipping options that include both domestic and cross-border shipping at discounted rates.
    - **Tracking**: Shipments made through the Partnered Carrier Program are automatically updated with tracking information.
3. **Freight Forwarders and Third-Party Carriers**: If you have large shipments, you might choose to use third-party freight forwarders or international logistics companies to send inventory to Amazon's FBA

centers. Amazon's FBA program allows you to choose from multiple carriers and routes.
- **Sea Freight or Air Freight**: For larger shipments, sea freight may be more cost-effective than air freight, but it takes longer. Ensure you balance cost and speed based on your needs.

Once your inventory is stored in the Amazon fulfillment centers of the target marketplace, Amazon takes over and handles the fulfillment, including shipping the products to international customers.

- **Amazon Global Store**: If you're selling on Amazon's U.S. marketplace, for example, you can use the **Amazon Global Store** program to make your products available for international buyers.
- **Export to International Markets**: You can enable **FBA Export**, which automatically makes your products available for customers in over 100 countries.

4. International FBA Fees

International shipping with FBA comes with additional fees that vary depending on the shipping method, destination country, and the size and weight of your products. Key fees include:

- **International Fulfillment Fees**: These fees are applied when orders are fulfilled from an international Amazon fulfillment center.

- **VAT Fees**: In countries that require VAT collection, you may need to pay VAT fees for storing inventory or selling in those countries.
- **Storage Fees**: If you're using FBA in international marketplaces, you'll be subject to Amazon's standard FBA storage fees based on the inventory stored in fulfillment centers.
- **Fulfillment Fees**: These fees depend on the size and weight of the product.
- **Storage Fees**: Based on the amount of space your products occupy in the FBA warehouse.
- **Long-Term Storage Fees**: If your inventory sits in an international warehouse for more than 365 days, you may incur long-term storage fees.

5. Managing Currency and Payments

Selling internationally requires managing multiple currencies. Amazon handles currency conversion for you and deposits earnings in your local currency. However, you'll need to account for:

- **Currency Conversion Fees**: Be mindful of any fees that might be charged for converting earnings from international sales to your local currency.
- **Tax Withholding**: Ensure you're familiar with tax obligations in the countries where you're selling.

6. Best Practices for International Shipping with FBA

- **Test New Markets**: Start with just one or two international marketplaces to gauge demand before expanding further.
- **Monitor Inventory Levels**: Use Amazon's **inventory reports** to track stock levels across different countries to ensure you don't run out of stock.
- **Use Amazon's Global Sales Analytics**: Take advantage of Amazon's reporting tools to track the performance of your products in various countries and optimize your strategy.
- **Consider International Promotions**: Offer region-specific promotions or discounts to attract customers in international markets.

International Shipping with Amazon FBA allows you to expand your business globally while relying on Amazon's robust fulfillment network. To get started, you need to join Amazon's Global Selling program, set up inventory in Amazon fulfillment centers in different regions, and manage international taxes and duties. Leveraging Amazon's **FBA Export** and **Partnered Carrier Program** helps save on international shipping costs, while Amazon handles order fulfillment, customs, and customer service. By carefully managing your inventory and costs, you can successfully grow your business in international markets with FBA.

Amazon's Customer Service for FBA Orders

Amazon's **Customer Service for FBA Orders** is designed to provide seamless support for both sellers and buyers, ensuring that FBA orders are processed smoothly and that any issues are resolved quickly. As a seller using Amazon FBA, you benefit from Amazon's robust customer service infrastructure, which handles most customer-facing concerns related to order fulfillment, returns, refunds, and other post-purchase issues.

1. Customer Service Responsibilities for FBA Sellers

When you use **Amazon FBA**, the majority of customer service responsibilities, particularly related to order fulfillment, are handled by Amazon. This includes:

- **Order Fulfillment**: Amazon handles the picking, packing, and shipping of products to customers from their fulfillment centers.
- **Returns and Refunds**: If a customer wants to return a product or request a refund, Amazon manages the return process, including issuing refunds according to their return policy.
- **Customer Inquiries**: For issues related to product information, shipping status, or general queries, Amazon's customer service team addresses the customer directly.

- **Customer Feedback**: Amazon also manages customer reviews and feedback for FBA products, ensuring that any product issues are handled according to their policies.

2. Amazon's Role in FBA Order Customer Service

While Amazon's customer service handles the bulk of the interaction, sellers are still involved in certain cases where issues cannot be resolved by Amazon directly. Here's a breakdown of the roles:

- **Order Status**: Amazon provides real-time tracking and delivery status updates to customers and sellers.
- **Customer Returns**: When a customer requests a return, Amazon processes the return, issues refunds, and communicates the necessary steps to the buyer.
- **Refunds and Replacements**: If the product is defective or damaged in transit, Amazon handles customer refund requests or product replacements, often without seller involvement.
- **Customer Communication**: For routine inquiries such as shipping delays, product queries, or general support, Amazon's customer service team handles these requests and communicates directly with the buyer.

- **Product Issues**: If a product has an issue, like quality defects or incorrect product descriptions, the seller is responsible for ensuring the issue is resolved in compliance with Amazon's policies.

- **Amazon Seller Performance**: While Amazon provides customer service, sellers are still accountable for maintaining high performance, including metrics like order defect rate, customer feedback, and returns.
- **Account Health**: Maintaining a healthy account with good customer satisfaction scores is important for sellers, as it impacts your ability to sell on Amazon.

3. Seller Support for FBA Orders

While Amazon handles the majority of customer-facing issues, there are situations where sellers need to get involved or seek assistance from Amazon's **Seller Support**. These include:

- **Product Defects or Issues**: If customers report defects or issues with your product, Amazon may reach out to you for clarification or action. You may need to offer an explanation or initiate a process to fix the problem.
- **Disputes**: If a customer has an issue that Amazon cannot resolve, you may need to step in and help mediate, especially in the case of negative feedback or product-related disputes.
- **Account Health Issues**: If your account is flagged for performance issues, including poor customer service metrics, you will need to address these concerns directly with Amazon's seller performance team.

1. **Contact Seller Support**:
   - For issues that require your attention, you can contact Amazon's Seller Support via **Seller Central**. Go to **Help** > **Contact Us** to start a case or chat with a

representative.
- When communicating with Seller Support, provide as much detail as possible about the issue (e.g., order number, product details, customer feedback) to speed up the resolution.
2. **Create and Manage Cases**:
    - If an issue arises (e.g., damaged inventory, order cancellation), you can open a support case in **Seller Central**. You'll be able to track the progress and updates directly in the case dashboard.
3. **Performance Metrics**:
    - Monitor your **Account Health** in **Seller Central** under **Performance** > **Account Health**. Keep track of customer complaints, returns, and other metrics to ensure your account remains in good standing.
    - Respond promptly to any performance notifications or requests for action from Amazon.

4. Handling FBA Returns and Refunds

Amazon handles most of the returns and refunds for FBA orders, but sellers need to be aware of Amazon's return policies and the potential impact on their business.

- **Return Window**: Amazon allows customers to return most products within **30 days** of receiving their order. However, there are exceptions depending on the category (e.g., electronics may have a 14-day return window).
- **Returns Processing**: When an item is returned, Amazon inspects the product to determine its condition. If the product is returned in sellable

condition, it is sent back to the fulfillment center; if damaged, it may be marked as unsellable.

- **Refunds**: Amazon automatically issues refunds to customers who return items in line with their return policy. If a return is approved, the customer gets a refund based on the original payment method.
- **Condition of Returned Items**: Amazon will automatically process returns, but you'll need to monitor the status and condition of returned items in **Seller Central**.
- **Return Reimbursement**: If the return is due to an issue with your product, Amazon will issue a refund. However, if the return is due to buyer's remorse or issues not related to the product, you may have to absorb the cost.
- **Restocking Fees**: Amazon charges restocking fees for certain returns, but FBA sellers are not responsible for these fees.

5. Handling Negative Feedback and Complaints

While Amazon handles most customer interactions, sellers are still responsible for maintaining a high level of customer satisfaction, which impacts their performance metrics.

- **Amazon's Policy on Reviews**: Amazon's customer service team manages feedback for FBA orders. If a customer leaves negative feedback due to fulfillment issues (e.g., late shipping, damaged items), Amazon may automatically remove the review.

- **Dispute Process**: If a review is not removed and you feel it violates Amazon's guidelines, you can appeal or respond to the review in a professional manner to mitigate its impact.

1. **Respond Promptly**: If a customer reaches out with a question or issue, respond as quickly as possible to maintain a good relationship.
2. **Be Proactive**: Stay on top of potential product issues. If you notice a pattern in customer complaints, investigate and address the problem quickly.
3. **Maintain Professionalism**: If you have to interact with customers (in rare cases), always keep your communication polite, helpful, and professional.

6. Amazon's Customer Service Tools for FBA Sellers

Amazon offers several tools to help FBA sellers manage customer service and track performance:

- **Performance Dashboard**: This provides an overview of your seller performance, including metrics such as **Order Defect Rate** (ODR), **Return Rate**, and **Customer Feedback**.
- **Customer Feedback Management**: From **Seller Central**, you can view feedback left by customers and take action if necessary (e.g., appealing negative reviews or addressing complaints).
- **Case Management**: Amazon provides tools for opening, managing, and resolving cases related to customer service issues or product concerns.

- **Return and Refund Reports**: You can view detailed reports on returns, refunds, and reimbursements in **Seller Central** to help track and resolve issues with returned products.

Amazon provides comprehensive customer service for FBA orders, handling most aspects of order fulfillment, returns, refunds, and customer inquiries. Sellers benefit from Amazon's robust customer support infrastructure, which ensures a smooth experience for buyers and frees sellers from many direct customer service tasks. However, sellers are still responsible for maintaining high performance and resolving specific issues related to product quality or customer complaints. By monitoring your **Account Health**, staying proactive about feedback, and using **Seller Central** to manage returns and inquiries, you can keep your FBA business running smoothly and maintain a good relationship with customers.

Managing Customer Feedback and Reviews

Managing Customer Feedback and Reviews is crucial for maintaining a positive reputation and ensuring the success of your Amazon FBA business. Feedback and reviews significantly impact your seller performance metrics, product visibility, and ultimately, sales. As a seller, it's important to actively monitor, respond to, and improve your feedback and reviews.

Here's how you can effectively manage customer feedback and reviews on Amazon:

1. Understanding Customer Feedback vs. Product Reviews

Before diving into managing feedback, it's important to distinguish between **Customer Feedback** and **Product Reviews**:

- **Customer Feedback**: This is an overall rating of your seller performance (e.g., 1-5 stars) left by buyers based on their entire shopping experience, including aspects like shipping speed, product quality, and communication.
  - **Feedback Categories**: Amazon separates customer feedback into **positive**, **neutral**, and **negative** categories.
  - **Impact**: Negative feedback can harm your seller rating and account health, while positive feedback boosts your reputation.
- **Product Reviews**: These are specific to individual products and are based on the buyer's experience with that product. Reviews can include ratings (1-5 stars) and comments about the product's quality, features, or functionality.
  - **Impact**: Product reviews directly affect your product's ranking and visibility on Amazon. Positive

reviews can lead to higher rankings in search results, while negative reviews can reduce sales.

2. Importance of Managing Customer Feedback and Reviews

- **Seller Reputation**: Positive feedback and reviews help build trust with new customers. Negative feedback can lead to lower trust and affect your sales.
- **Performance Metrics**: Amazon tracks various performance metrics, such as **Order Defect Rate (ODR)**, **Late Shipment Rate**, and **Customer Feedback Score**. Poor performance in these areas can lead to account suspension or restrictions.
- **Customer Trust and Sales**: Reviews directly influence product visibility in search results, affecting conversion rates. The more positive reviews, the more likely customers are to purchase your product.

3. Monitoring Customer Feedback and Product Reviews

Regularly checking and responding to feedback and reviews is essential for managing your Amazon presence.

- **Seller Central**: You can access customer feedback through **Seller Central** under the **Performance** tab. Here, you can view all the feedback left by buyers.
- **Feedback Reports**: Amazon provides a detailed **Feedback Report** in Seller Central, where you can filter by date and review types (positive, neutral, or negative).

- **Notifications**: You can set up notifications in Seller Central to receive alerts when new feedback or reviews are posted.
- **Product Reviews Dashboard**: In Seller Central, you can view **Product Reviews** through the **Customer Reviews** section. This lets you see the reviews for all your products.
- **Amazon Review Requests**: You can send requests for reviews through **Request a Review** in Seller Central. However, it's important to note that you cannot incentivize or solicit reviews in an unethical manner, like offering discounts in exchange for reviews.

4. Responding to Customer Feedback and Product Reviews

Amazon allows sellers to interact with customers via both feedback and product reviews, although there are some restrictions.

- **Respond to Negative Feedback**: If you receive negative feedback, you have the option to respond to the customer's comments. This response can help resolve the issue and show potential customers that you care about their experience.

    - **Apologize and Offer a Solution**: Be polite and professional when responding. Apologize for the issue, acknowledge the customer's concern, and offer a solution (e.g., refund, replacement, or explanation).
    - **Use Seller Central to Respond**: You can respond to feedback directly in Seller Central under the **Customer Feedback** section.

- **Ask for Removal of Unfair Feedback**: If you feel the feedback is unfair or violates Amazon's policies (e.g., based on an incorrect order or product description), you can request its removal from **Seller Central**.

- **Requesting Feedback**: You can encourage customers to leave feedback after their purchase, but Amazon strictly prohibits incentivizing feedback. Use **Amazon's Feedback Request tool** to send an automatic request for feedback after an order is delivered.

- **Responding to Reviews**: Amazon allows sellers to respond to product reviews publicly. This is an opportunity to thank customers for their feedback, apologize for any dissatisfaction, and clarify any misunderstandings.

  - **Apologies and Resolution**: If a customer leaves a negative review, you can offer to resolve the issue, e.g., by providing a replacement or refund. Keep responses polite and professional.
  - **No Incentives**: You cannot ask for reviews or offer incentives to customers in exchange for a positive review.

- **Managing Negative Reviews**: While you cannot directly delete or modify a product review, you can:
  - **Report Violations**: If a review violates Amazon's guidelines (e.g., contains inappropriate content, is unrelated to the product, or is biased), you can report it through Seller Central.

- **Address the Issue**: If a review indicates a product or service issue, investigate the cause. If it's a genuine complaint (e.g., defective product), take corrective action, such as improving product quality or addressing the customer's complaint.

5. Proactive Strategies to Improve Feedback and Reviews

While you cannot control what customers write in their reviews, you can take steps to improve your feedback and review scores.

- **Quality Control**: Ensure that your products are high quality and meet the descriptions provided in your listings. A high-quality product reduces the likelihood of negative feedback.
- **Accurate Listings**: Be clear and honest about your product's features, specifications, and condition. This helps manage customer expectations and reduce complaints.
- **Packaging and Shipping**: Ensure your products are well-packaged and shipped promptly. Delays or damaged products often lead to negative reviews.
- **Responsive Communication**: If customers reach out with questions or concerns, respond promptly and professionally. A quick resolution can prevent negative feedback.
- **Handling Returns and Refunds**: Make the returns and refund process as easy as possible for customers. A hassle-free return process often leads to better feedback, even if the customer didn't keep the product.

- **Use Amazon's "Request a Review" Feature**: After a customer receives their order, you can use Amazon's automated **Request a Review** tool to ask them to leave feedback and a product review. This can increase the likelihood of receiving positive reviews.

- **Third-Party Tools**: Some third-party tools integrate with Seller Central to automate review requests, though always stay within Amazon's guidelines regarding review solicitation.
- **Shipping Efficiency**: Fast and reliable shipping improves customer satisfaction. Use Amazon's **FBA** program to ensure quick and reliable order fulfillment.
- **Professional Packaging**: Ensure your packaging is durable and presentable. This enhances the customer's experience and reduces the likelihood of complaints about damaged products.

6. Handling Negative Feedback or Reviews

If negative feedback or reviews arise, it's important to address them professionally and swiftly:

- **Responding to Negative Feedback**: Always respond to negative feedback in a constructive way. Address the specific concern, offer an apology, and explain how you plan to resolve the issue.
- **Following Up on Resolutions**: If you resolve the issue for the customer (e.g., issuing a refund or sending a replacement), ask if they would consider updating or

removing their review. However, Amazon prohibits requesting review removals in exchange for incentives.
- **Monitoring Your Account Health**: Negative feedback can hurt your **Order Defect Rate (ODR)** and **Customer Feedback Rating**. Monitor these metrics and take action to resolve customer issues quickly.

7. Using Reviews to Improve Your Business

- **Product Development**: Use customer reviews as valuable feedback for improving your products. If you notice recurring complaints about a feature, consider making improvements to future versions of the product.
- **Customer Engagement**: Engaging with customers and addressing their concerns builds customer loyalty and may encourage them to leave a positive review in the future.
- **Reputation Management**: Regularly monitor your feedback and reviews, and address issues as they arise to keep your reputation strong.

Managing **Customer Feedback and Product Reviews** on Amazon is vital for the success of your FBA business. Regularly monitor feedback and reviews, respond to negative comments professionally, and ensure that you provide excellent customer service to maintain high ratings. By proactively improving product quality, delivery, and customer interactions, you can minimize negative feedback and increase positive reviews, ultimately boosting your seller reputation and product visibility.

Ensuring FBA Account Health

Ensuring FBA Account Health is critical for maintaining your ability to sell on Amazon, particularly as an FBA (Fulfilled by Amazon) seller. Amazon uses several performance metrics to evaluate sellers, and maintaining healthy performance is essential to avoid penalties, account suspension, or even termination. Regularly monitoring and improving these metrics will help ensure your account stays in good standing.

1. Key Account Health Metrics

Amazon evaluates FBA sellers based on the following key performance metrics:

- **What It Is**: ODR is a percentage of orders with negative feedback, A-to-Z claims, or credit card chargebacks.
- **Why It Matters**: A high ODR indicates poor customer satisfaction and can lead to account suspension. Amazon requires sellers to maintain an ODR of **less than 1%**.
- **How to Improve It**:

Respond promptly to customer complaints or issues.

Resolve A-to-Z claims efficiently and fairly.

Monitor customer feedback to address issues before they escalate.

- **What It Is**: LSR measures the percentage of orders that are shipped after the promised ship date.
- **Why It Matters**: A high LSR signals delays in fulfilling orders, which can negatively impact the customer experience. Sellers are required to maintain an LSR of **less than 4%**.
- **How to Improve It**:
  Ensure timely dispatch of orders, particularly during busy times (holidays, promotions).

  Use Amazon's **FBA** program, which handles storage, picking, packing, and shipping to reduce the risk of delays.

  Set realistic ship dates to avoid missing deadlines.

- **What It Is**: The percentage of orders that are canceled before they are fulfilled (by the seller).
- **Why It Matters**: A high cancel rate can signal inventory issues or a lack of reliability in fulfilling orders. A **rate above 2.5%** can hurt your account health.

- **How to Improve It**:

  Keep inventory levels updated in Seller Central to avoid selling out-of-stock items.

  Use Amazon's **FBA** service to handle inventory management and prevent cancellations due to stockouts.

  Ensure that product availability is accurately reflected in your listings.

- **What It Is**: This metric tracks how often customers are dissatisfied with the return process.
- **Why It Matters**: A high dissatisfaction rate can indicate poor customer service or unprocessed returns, leading to account health issues.
- **How to Improve It**:

  Use Amazon's **FBA** return processing, which automates returns and issues refunds swiftly.

  Provide clear return policies and instructions for customers.

  Respond to return requests promptly and fairly.

- **What It Is**: This is an overall rating based on customer feedback on your seller performance, such as shipping speed and communication.

- **Why It Matters**: A low rating can hurt your seller reputation. Amazon requires sellers to maintain a feedback rating of **at least 90% positive**.
- **How to Improve It**:

  Respond quickly to customer inquiries and complaints.

  Ensure high-quality, accurate product listings.

  Aim for fast and reliable delivery by using **FBA**.

- **What It Is**: These notifications are issued by Amazon when your account violates performance standards.
- **Why It Matters**: Ignoring these warnings can lead to account suspension.
- **How to Improve It**:

  Monitor **Seller Central** regularly for any account health notifications.

  Respond promptly to Amazon's requests for action, and provide the necessary information to resolve any issues.

2. How to Monitor and Track Account Health

Regular monitoring of your account's performance is crucial to avoid unexpected issues.

- **Account Health Dashboard**: Seller Central provides an **Account Health** dashboard under the **Performance**

tab. This dashboard tracks your key metrics, such as ODR, LSR, and customer feedback.
- **Notifications and Alerts**: Amazon sends performance alerts via Seller Central when any of your metrics fall below required thresholds.
- **Reports**: Download reports related to returns, late shipments, and feedback to identify areas for improvement. Regularly review your
- **Seller Performance** tab in Seller Central to track your ODR, LSR, and other critical metrics.
- **Performance Notifications**: Set up notifications to get alerts when performance issues arise so that you can address them promptly.

3. Best Practices for Maintaining FBA Account Health

- **Respond to Negative Feedback**: Always respond to negative feedback in a polite and professional manner. Offer solutions, such as refunds, replacements, or other remedies, and try to turn the negative experience into a positive one.
- **Monitor Reviews**: If feedback seems unwarranted or unfair, follow Amazon's procedures for disputing and removing inappropriate feedback.
- **FBA Inventory Management**: Amazon's FBA service handles storage, packaging, and shipping, which significantly reduces the risk of missing shipment deadlines or incorrect handling of orders.
- **FBA Tracking and Reporting**: Use FBA tools in **Seller Central** to track inventory levels, shipping status, and

customer returns. This can help you stay proactive in managing your FBA account.
- **Stock Levels**: Keep inventory stocked appropriately to avoid canceling orders due to stockouts, which will help prevent a high **Pre-Fulfillment Cancel Rate**.
- **Replenishment**: Regularly check for stock levels and plan for replenishment early to avoid running out of popular items.
- **Inventory Health**: Periodically audit your inventory to ensure that all products are sellable and in good condition.
- **Reliable Shipping**: Always meet your shipping deadlines, or use Amazon FBA to ensure that your products are shipped quickly and reliably.
- **Promised Ship Dates**: Be realistic about your ship dates, especially if you're handling your fulfillment. If you cannot fulfill an order on time, cancel it proactively before the buyer notices.
- **Handle Claims Quickly**: A high rate of A-to-Z claims can negatively affect your account health. Ensure that any claims related to late delivery, defective products, or missing items are handled quickly and fairly.
- **Prevention**: Minimize the chance of claims by providing accurate product descriptions, clear images, and proper fulfillment procedures.
- **Communicate with Buyers**: Always maintain a professional tone when communicating with customers. If they have questions or issues, respond promptly and professionally.

- **Resolve Issues Quickly**: If a customer raises a concern, such as a missing item or product defect, resolve it quickly to avoid disputes or negative feedback.
- **Return and Refund Policy**: Clearly state your return and refund policies, especially if you're handling fulfillment yourself. Provide a smooth return process for customers to avoid dissatisfaction.

4. Reacting to Account Health Warnings

If you receive an **Account Health Notification** or warning from Amazon, it's essential to address the issue quickly to prevent account suspension.

- **Investigate the Cause**: Identify the root cause of the performance issue (e.g., high ODR, late shipments, or negative feedback).
- **Create a Plan of Action (POA)**: If Amazon notifies you of an issue, you will likely need to submit a Plan of Action (POA) outlining how you intend to resolve the problem. Your POA should:

    Identify the issue (e.g., shipping delays, inventory issues).

    Explain what steps you have taken or will take to address the problem (e.g., improve inventory management, streamline shipping processes).

    Provide proof of corrective actions (e.g., new procedures, inventory audits).

Maintaining **FBA Account Health** requires regular monitoring and proactive management of key metrics such as Order Defect Rate (ODR), Late Shipment Rate (LSR), and customer feedback. By addressing issues quickly, utilizing Amazon's FBA services for fulfillment, and providing excellent customer service, you can ensure that your account remains in good standing. Monitoring performance via **Seller Central**, maintaining inventory, and adhering to Amazon's guidelines will help you sustain a healthy account, avoid penalties, and continue growing your business on Amazon.

Leveraging FBA for Prime Eligibility

Leveraging Amazon's Fulfillment by Amazon (FBA) service is a strategic approach to ensure your products are Prime-eligible, thereby enhancing their visibility and appeal to a vast customer base. Here's how FBA facilitates Prime eligibility and the benefits it offers:

1. Automatic Prime Eligibility with FBA

When you enroll your products in FBA, Amazon handles the storage, packing, and shipping from its fulfillment centers. This integration automatically qualifies your products for Prime benefits, including free Two-Day Shipping for Prime members. The Prime badge displayed on your listings signifies fast and reliable delivery, which can significantly boost customer trust and conversion rates.

2. Enhanced Customer Trust and Sales Potential

The Prime badge is a marker of quality and reliability. Products with this badge are more likely to be chosen by customers seeking swift delivery and dependable service. By utilizing FBA, you not only gain Prime eligibility but also benefit from Amazon's robust customer service and return handling, further enhancing the customer experience.

3. Simplified Logistics and Focus on Growth

FBA streamlines your logistics by managing inventory storage, order fulfillment, and customer service. This allows you to focus on other critical aspects of your business, such as product development and marketing, while Amazon ensures efficient delivery and customer satisfaction.

4. Cost Considerations

While FBA offers numerous advantages, it's important to assess the associated fees, which include storage and fulfillment costs. These fees vary based on product size, weight, and storage duration. Conducting a cost-benefit analysis will help determine if FBA aligns with your business model and profitability goals.

5. Alternative: Seller Fulfilled Prime (SFP)

If you prefer to manage your own fulfillment while still offering Prime benefits, Amazon's Seller Fulfilled Prime (SFP) program is an alternative. SFP allows you to fulfill orders from your own warehouse while displaying the Prime badge, provided you meet Amazon's stringent performance requirements, including fast shipping and excellent customer service.

Enrolling in FBA is a straightforward method to make your products Prime-eligible, thereby enhancing their attractiveness to customers and potentially increasing sales. However, it's crucial to evaluate the associated costs and consider whether FBA or SFP better suits your business needs and operational capabilities.

Advertising and Driving Traffic to FBA Products

Advertising and Driving Traffic to FBA Products is a critical strategy for increasing visibility and sales on Amazon. By leveraging Amazon's advertising tools and external marketing methods, you can attract potential buyers to your product listings and boost their performance.

Benefits of Advertising for FBA Products

- **Increased Visibility**: Advertising positions your product prominently on search result pages and product detail pages.
- **Higher Sales**: Ads can help convert browsing shoppers into buyers.
- **Boost Organic Ranking**: A well-performing ad campaign can improve your product's organic ranking, leading to long-term sales growth.

Amazon Ads offers a suite of advertising solutions designed to help businesses of all sizes reach and engage customers throughout their purchasing journey. These solutions include:

- **Sponsored Products**: Cost-per-click (CPC) ads that promote individual product listings, enhancing visibility in shopping results and on product detail pages.
- **Sponsored Brands**: Ads featuring your brand logo, a custom headline, and multiple products or a video, aimed at boosting brand awareness and driving discovery.
- **Sponsored Display**: Display ads that reach relevant audiences both on and off Amazon, helping to re-engage shoppers and drive product consideration.
- **Amazon DSP (Demand-Side Platform)**: Enables programmatic buying of display, video, and audio ads to reach audiences across Amazon sites and apps, as well as through third-party exchanges.

- **Video and Audio Ads**: Formats that allow brands to tell their stories through streaming TV, online video, and audio ads, connecting with customers during their entertainment experiences.

Promotions and Deals for FBA Sellers

As an Amazon FBA (Fulfillment by Amazon) seller, leveraging various promotional tools can significantly enhance your product visibility and boost sales. Here's an overview of the primary promotional options available:

1. Deals

- **Lightning Deals**: These are time-sensitive promotions where your product is featured on Amazon's Deals page for a few hours. To participate, you must have a Professional selling plan, an overall rating of at least four stars, and meet specific product eligibility criteria. There's a fee associated with each Lightning Deal, typically around $150, though it can increase during peak events like Prime Day.
- **7-Day Deals**: Similar to Lightning Deals but with a longer duration, these promotions run for up to seven days, providing extended exposure on the Deals page.

The eligibility criteria are akin to Lightning Deals, and the fee is generally higher due to the extended visibility.

2. Promotions

- **Percentage-Off Promotions**: Offer customers a discount based on a percentage off the product price. This can be structured to encourage higher order values, such as "Buy two, get 20% off."
- **Buy One, Get One (BOGO) Promotions**: Entice customers by offering a free or discounted item when they purchase a specified product. For example, "Buy one, get one 50% off."
- **Social Media Promo Codes**: Create unique discount codes to share via social media platforms or with specific influencers, driving targeted traffic to your listings.

3. Coupons

Coupons are discounts that appear directly on your product listings, marked with a distinctive badge, making them highly visible to potential buyers. Customers can "clip" these coupons and apply them at checkout. To create a coupon, you need a Professional selling plan and an overall seller rating of at least 3.5 stars. Amazon charges a fee of $0.60 for each coupon redeemed, and there's a minimum budget requirement of $100.

4. Prime Exclusive Discounts

These are special discounts available only to Prime members, often utilized during major sales events like Prime Day. To offer a Prime Exclusive Discount, your product must be Prime-eligible, have a minimum 3.5-star rating, and meet other specific criteria.

Best Practices for Implementing Promotions

- **Plan Ahead**: Schedule your promotions in advance, especially for major sales events, to ensure adequate inventory and optimal timing.
- **Monitor Performance**: Regularly assess the effectiveness of your promotions by tracking key metrics such as sales volume, conversion rates, and return on investment.
- **Optimize Listings**: Ensure your product listings are optimized with high-quality images, detailed descriptions, and relevant keywords to maximize the impact of your promotions.

By strategically utilizing these promotional tools, you can enhance your product's visibility, attract more customers, and ultimately drive higher sales on Amazon.

Using Multi-Channel Fulfillment (MCF)

Amazon's **Multi-Channel Fulfillment (MCF)** allows FBA sellers to leverage Amazon's fulfillment network to store, pick, pack, and ship orders for sales made through channels outside Amazon, such as your website or other e-commerce platforms. This service provides flexibility for businesses operating across multiple sales channels while maintaining efficient inventory management and quick delivery. Here's a detailed overview:

Key Features of MCF

1. **Access to Amazon's Fulfillment Network**
   Utilize Amazon's vast network for fast and reliable shipping, with options like one-day, two-day, and standard delivery.
2. **Brand-Neutral Packaging**
   Orders fulfilled through MCF are shipped in plain, non-branded packaging, so your customers won't see Amazon branding unless you opt otherwise.
3. **Integration with Other Platforms**
   Amazon MCF integrates with major e-commerce platforms like Shopify, BigCommerce, and WooCommerce, allowing seamless order management.
4. **Real-Time Tracking**
   MCF provides real-time tracking updates, ensuring customers can monitor the progress of their shipments.

5. **Flexible Shipping Options**
   Choose from multiple shipping speeds:

   - Standard (3-5 business days)
   - Expedited (2 business days)
   - Priority (1 business day)

Benefits of Using MCF

- **Simplified Operations**
  Centralize inventory management for all your sales channels in one place.
- **Scalability**
  Leverage Amazon's logistics infrastructure during peak sales periods without the need for additional storage or labor.
- **Improved Customer Experience**
  Quick and reliable shipping enhances your brand's reputation and boosts customer satisfaction.
- **Cost Efficiency**
  Save on warehousing and logistics by using Amazon's network, particularly for businesses without dedicated fulfillment teams.

How to Set Up MCF

1. **Inventory Management**
   Store your inventory in Amazon's fulfillment centers by creating inbound shipments in Seller Central.
2. **Create Orders**
   Submit MCF orders manually through Seller Central,

via bulk uploads, or using API integrations for automated processing.
3. **Track Orders**
Monitor fulfillment progress and shipping through the MCF dashboard or integrated e-commerce platform.

Fees for MCF

MCF charges depend on factors such as shipping speed, item dimensions, and weight. Fees are generally higher than standard FBA fees due to the multi-channel nature.

- **Fulfillment Fee**: Covers the cost of picking, packing, and shipping.
- **Storage Fee**: Charged monthly based on the cubic feet your inventory occupies.
- **Additional Costs**: Special handling for oversized items or inventory removal.

To calculate fees, use Amazon's **MCF Fee Calculator** in Seller Central.

Best Practices for Using MCF

1. **Optimize Inventory Levels**
Maintain a balance to prevent stockouts for all channels while minimizing storage fees.
2. **Sync Your Platforms**
Use inventory management tools or software that sync across channels to avoid overselling.

3. **Leverage Bulk Fulfillment**
   For peak sales events, use bulk uploads to save time and streamline order processing.
4. **Monitor Profit Margins**
   Regularly analyze costs to ensure MCF fees are sustainable for your business model.
5. **Provide Accurate Shipping Times**
   Clearly communicate delivery times based on the chosen shipping speed to set customer expectations.

MCF vs. FBA

Feature	MCF	FBA
Channels Served	External (non-Amazon) + Amazon	Amazon only
Branding Options	Plain packaging (brand-neutral)	Amazon-branded packaging
Cost	Typically higher fees for non-Amazon channels	Competitive fees within Amazon ecosystem

By utilizing Amazon MCF, you can streamline operations, expand your reach, and provide excellent service to customers across multiple platforms.

Scaling Your Business with FBA

Scaling your Amazon FBA (Fulfillment by Amazon) business involves strategic planning and execution to enhance growth and profitability. Here are key strategies to consider:

1. Expand Your Product Line

Introducing new products that align with your brand can attract a broader customer base and increase sales. Conduct thorough market research to identify high-demand items and assess competition. Utilize tools like Amazon's Best Sellers and Trending Products sections to gauge potential demand and stay ahead of market shifts.

2. Optimize Product Listings

Enhance your product listings to improve visibility and conversion rates:

- **Keyword Optimization**: Incorporate relevant keywords in titles, bullet points, and descriptions to improve search rankings.
- **High-Quality Images**: Use clear, high-resolution images that showcase your product from multiple angles.
- **Compelling Descriptions**: Highlight key features and benefits to persuade potential buyers.

Regularly updating your listings based on keyword trends and customer feedback will keep them relevant and effective.

3. Implement Effective Marketing Strategies

Boost your product's visibility and sales through targeted marketing:

- **Amazon Advertising**: Utilize Sponsored Products, Sponsored Brands, and Sponsored Display ads to reach potential customers.
- **External Traffic**: Drive traffic from social media, email marketing, and other channels to your Amazon listings.
- **Promotions and Deals**: Offer discounts, coupons, and limited-time deals to incentivize purchases.

Marketing is crucial for scaling your Amazon FBA business to higher revenue levels.

4. Enhance Inventory Management

Efficient inventory management ensures product availability and reduces storage costs:

- **Demand Forecasting**: Analyze sales data to predict future demand and adjust inventory levels accordingly.
- **Reorder Alerts**: Set up notifications to reorder stock before it runs low.

- **Storage Optimization**: Monitor storage fees and adjust inventory to minimize costs.

Never stocking out is essential to maintain sales momentum and customer satisfaction.

5. Expand to International Markets

Reaching customers in other countries can significantly increase your market size:

- **Amazon Global Selling**: Utilize Amazon's international marketplaces to sell your products globally.
- **Compliance**: Understand and adhere to international regulations, taxes, and shipping requirements.

Expanding to Amazon Europe or Amazon UK requires more research, including understanding the best fulfillment setup and tax regulations.

6. Automate and Outsource Operations

Streamline your business processes to focus on growth:

- **Automation Tools**: Use software for tasks like repricing, feedback management, and inventory tracking.
- **Outsourcing**: Delegate tasks such as customer service, content creation, and advertising management to professionals.

By implementing these strategies, you can effectively scale your Amazon FBA business, increase revenue, and build a sustainable brand.

FBA for Private Label and Wholesale

Ensuring product safety is paramount for both private label and wholesale sellers utilizing Amazon's Fulfillment by Amazon (FBA) service. Adherence to Amazon's safety standards not only protects consumers but also maintains your seller account's good standing. Below are key safety requirements and best practices for FBA sellers:

1. Compliance with Regulatory Standards

- **Product Safety Regulations**: Ensure your products comply with all relevant safety standards and regulations applicable in the target market. This includes certifications such as CE marking in Europe or UL listing in the United States.
- **Testing and Certification**: Conduct necessary product testing through accredited laboratories to verify compliance. Maintain documentation of all certifications and test reports.

2. Accurate Labeling and Documentation

- **Product Labels**: Include all required information on product labels, such as safety warnings, usage instructions, and manufacturer details. For private label products, ensure your brand name and contact information are clearly displayed.
- **Documentation**: Provide comprehensive user manuals and safety instructions with your products. Keep digital copies accessible for reference and customer support.

3. Packaging Requirements

- **Protective Packaging**: Use appropriate packaging materials to safeguard products during transit and storage. Fragile items should have sufficient cushioning to prevent damage.
- **Poly Bags**: If using poly bags, they must be at least 1.5 mil thick and transparent. Bags larger than 5 inches require a suffocation warning label. Ensure the barcode is scannable through the bag or place an additional label on the outside.

4. Barcode and Labeling Compliance

- **FNSKU Labels**: Each unit must have a unique Fulfillment Network Stock Keeping Unit (FNSKU) label. Labels should be printed on a white background, at least 0.25 inches in height, and placed over any existing barcodes.

- **Label Placement**: Affix labels on a flat surface of the product or packaging where they are easily scannable and not obscured by seams or edges.

5. Hazardous Materials (Hazmat) Compliance

- **Hazmat Identification**: Determine if your products are classified as hazardous materials. This includes items like batteries, aerosols, or flammable substances.
- **Proper Handling**: Follow Amazon's guidelines for shipping and storing hazmat items, including appropriate labeling and packaging.

6. Monitoring and Recalls

- **Product Monitoring**: Regularly review customer feedback and returns to identify potential safety issues.
- **Recall Procedures**: Establish a clear process for handling product recalls, including prompt communication with Amazon and customers, and removal of affected inventory.

By diligently adhering to these safety requirements, FBA sellers can ensure their products meet Amazon's standards, thereby protecting consumers and sustaining a successful selling account.

FBA Product Compliance and Safety Requirements

Ensuring product compliance and safety is crucial for sellers utilizing Amazon's Fulfillment by Amazon (FBA) service. Adhering to Amazon's guidelines and relevant regulations helps maintain customer trust and prevents potential account issues. Below is an overview of key compliance and safety requirements for FBA sellers:

1. Compliance with Regulatory Standards

- **Product Safety Regulations**: Ensure your products meet all applicable safety standards and regulations in the target market. This includes obtaining necessary certifications and conducting product testing to verify compliance.
- **Documentation**: Maintain up-to-date documentation, such as safety data sheets, test reports, and certificates of conformity, to demonstrate compliance when requested.

2. Accurate Labeling and Documentation

- **Product Labels**: Include all required information on product labels, such as safety warnings, usage instructions, and manufacturer details. For private label products, ensure your brand name and contact information are clearly displayed.

- **Documentation**: Provide comprehensive user manuals and safety instructions with your products. Keep digital copies accessible for reference and customer support.

3. Packaging Requirements

- **Protective Packaging**: Use appropriate packaging materials to safeguard products during transit and storage. Fragile items should have sufficient cushioning to prevent damage.
- **Poly Bags**: If using poly bags, they must be at least 1.5 mil thick and transparent. Bags larger than 5 inches require a suffocation warning label. Ensure the barcode is scannable through the bag or place an additional label on the outside.

4. Barcode and Labeling Compliance

- **FNSKU Labels**: Each unit must have a unique Fulfillment Network Stock Keeping Unit (FNSKU) label. Labels should be printed on a white background, at least 0.25 inches in height, and placed over any existing barcodes.
- **Label Placement**: Affix labels on a flat surface of the product or packaging where they are easily scannable and not obscured by seams or edges.

5. Hazardous Materials (Hazmat) Compliance

- **Hazmat Identification**: Determine if your products are classified as hazardous materials. This includes items like batteries, aerosols, or flammable substances.
- **Proper Handling**: Follow Amazon's guidelines for shipping and storing hazmat items, including appropriate labeling and packaging.

6. Monitoring and Recalls

- **Product Monitoring**: Regularly review customer feedback and returns to identify potential safety issues.
- **Recall Procedures**: Establish a clear process for handling product recalls, including prompt communication with Amazon and customers, and removal of affected inventory.

By diligently adhering to these safety requirements, FBA sellers can ensure their products meet Amazon's standards, thereby protecting consumers and sustaining a successful selling account.

Analyzing FBA Performance Reports

Analyzing Fulfillment by Amazon (FBA) performance reports is crucial for understanding your business's efficiency, profitability, and customer satisfaction. These reports provide valuable insights to help you optimize operations and make data-driven decisions.

Key FBA Performance Reports

1. **Sales Reports**

    Metrics Tracked: Units sold, revenue generated, and average selling price.

    Insights: Identify high-performing products and seasonal trends.

    Actions: Adjust inventory and marketing strategies based on sales performance.

2. **Inventory Reports**

    Available Reports: Inventory Age Report, Restock Inventory Report, and Excess Inventory Report.

    Metrics Tracked: Inventory levels, aging stock, and storage fees.

    Insights: Recognize slow-moving inventory to reduce long-term storage fees.

Actions: Optimize inventory turnover by running promotions or adjusting prices.

3. **Returns Reports**

   Metrics Tracked: Return reasons, defective units, and customer complaints.

   Insights: Detect patterns in returns to identify product or fulfillment issues.

   Actions: Improve product quality or clarify descriptions to reduce returns.

4. **Fee Reports**

   Metrics Tracked: Fulfillment fees, storage fees, and other charges.

   Insights: Assess profitability by understanding how fees impact margins.

   Actions: Evaluate pricing strategies and product dimensions to lower costs.

5. **Customer Feedback Reports**

   Metrics Tracked: Ratings, reviews, and customer complaints.

   Insights: Gauge customer satisfaction and identify areas needing improvement.

Actions: Address negative feedback promptly and implement suggested improvements.

6. **Shipment Reports**

    Metrics Tracked: Inbound shipment status, discrepancies, and carrier performance.

    Insights: Monitor inventory replenishment efficiency.

    Actions: Adjust shipping timelines or work with reliable carriers to avoid delays.

7. **Performance Dashboard**

    Metrics Tracked: Account health metrics such as order defect rate, late shipment rate, and valid tracking rate.

    Insights: Ensure compliance with Amazon's performance standards.

    Actions: Take corrective actions promptly to maintain account health

---

Profitability with FBA

Calculating profitability with Fulfillment by Amazon (FBA) involves assessing all costs and revenues to determine your net profit for each product and your overall business. Here's a step-by-step guide to evaluate profitability effectively:

Key Metrics for Calculating Profitability

1. **Revenue**

    Selling Price: The price at which your product is sold on Amazon.

    Units Sold: The quantity of products sold during a specific period.

2. **FBA Fees**

    Referral Fee: A percentage of the product's selling price (typically 6%-15%, depending on the category).

    Fulfillment Fee: Charges for storage, picking, packing, and shipping products.

    Storage Fees: Monthly storage fees based on the volume and duration of stored inventory.

    Other Fees: Returns processing fees, disposal fees, or overage charges.

3. **Cost of Goods Sold (COGS)**

    The total cost of manufacturing or purchasing the product, including packaging.

4. **Advertising Costs**

    Expenses for Amazon PPC campaigns and external marketing efforts.

5. **Shipping Costs (Inbound to FBA)**

    Charges incurred for sending inventory to Amazon's fulfillment centers.

6. **Other Expenses**

    Includes software subscriptions, professional photography, or any additional operational costs.

Tools for Calculating FBA Profitability

1. **Amazon FBA Revenue Calculator**
    - Available in Amazon Seller Central to estimate fees and profits per product.
2. **Third-Party Tools**
    - Use tools like Jungle Scout, Helium 10, or AMZScout for detailed profitability analysis.
3. **Spreadsheets**
    - Maintain a custom Excel or Google Sheets file for tracking and calculating costs and profits.

Tips for Maximizing Profitability

1. **Optimize Pricing**
   - Regularly review your competitors' prices and adjust your pricing strategy to maximize revenue without sacrificing margins.
2. **Reduce COGS**
   - Negotiate with suppliers for lower costs or explore bulk purchasing.
3. **Minimize Advertising Costs**
   - Use data-driven campaigns to improve ROI and reduce wasteful spending.
4. **Efficient Inventory Management**
   - Avoid overstocking to reduce storage fees and prevent long-term storage costs.
5. **Bundle Products**
   - Increase average order value by offering product bundles or kits.

By carefully calculating and monitoring these factors, you can gain a clear understanding of your FBA profitability and identify opportunities to improve your business performance.

NOTE

It's essential to stay informed about Amazon's policies and guidelines related to customer communication, marketing, and promotions as they may evolve over time. Always ensure that your strategies align with Amazon's terms of service. For the most current and accurate information, refer to Amazon's official documentation and seller guidelines.

DISCLAIMER:

This book refers to the term "Amazon" for training & education purposes only. The use of the name "Amazon" is not intended to claim any ownership, affiliation, or endorsement by Amazon or its parent company, Amazon.com the Amazon name mentioned in this book is the exclusive property of Amazon.com. All rights to the Amazon name, logo, and trademark are acknowledged and belong solely to Amazon.com.

This book is not authorized, endorsed, or affiliated with Amazon or Amazon.com. It is designed for educational and training purposes only. Any references made to Amazon are used descriptively and are not intended to infringe upon the intellectual property rights of Amazon.com.

www.ingramcontent.com/pod-product-compliance
Lightning Source LLC
Chambersburg PA
CBHW071038240526
45469CB00006BD/2255